Loves Eternal Dance

Poetry From The Heart

LOVE'S ETERNAL DANCE

First edition. February 9, 2024.

ISBN: 979-8224817726

Written by Teri Dourmashkin.

For those who have loved and lost, who have known both joy and sorrow, and who continue to find beauty in the tapestry of life's moments.May these poems offer you comfort, reflection, and a reminder that you are not alone on this journey of the heart.~ Teri

☾ Loves Eternal Dance ☽

Your words of love penetrate my heart.
Time for new chapters, old books fall apart.
Come take my hand, let's dance at twilight.
Whispers of romance, finest French art.
Your passion otherworldly, soft meteorite.
Get lost in my essence two worlds not apart.

☾ Poetry From The Heart ☽

Lives often torn so much heartache.
Gaze past the veneer tears dressed in disguise.
Souls that are hurting please don't forsake.
Depression so deep blackest of skies.
Trembling, crawling, shivers, and shakes.
Unleash your compassion let us all rise.

****☽ Loves Eternal Dance ☾****

Pain has a language all its own.
Thunderous bolt lightening and moans.
Buried beneath in caverns unknown.
The brain believes it knows what's best.
Parts so primitive on its own quest.
Tossed around weary, windblown,
Angel's whisper, "You'll heal don't bemoan."

****☾ Poetry From The Heart ☽****

Your fingers caressing my windswept hair.
My body lifted rarefied air.
Pain evaporating, inky clouds whisk away.
Chopin sonatas starlight in my ears.
Your love a gift, French chocolates I sway.
Kiss me for hours, come dry up my tears.

****☾ Loves Eternal Dance ☽****

Can love pierce the barrier of physical space?
Can it be truly felt without a bodily embrace?
Can hearts feel connected down to their cores?
Can friendship or romance feel divine grace?
Yes, love is transcendent to you I adore.

☾ Poetry From The Heart ☽

Life is a journey or, so we've been told.
One lifetime to another missing pages of books.
Glimmers of images begin to unfold.
Lessons still to be learned take a good look.
The weight may feel daunting shivering cold.
All in divine timing soft trickling brook.

❨ Loves Eternal Dance ❩

Pain sometimes a mystery decades old art.
You speak your own language worlds so apart.
What are you telling me, talk to my heart?
Screaming five alarm fire need a new start.
Want a translator such foreign tongues.
Feeling so weary have I only begun?

☾ Poetry From The Heart ☽

True friendship a gift precious and rare.
Flows through calm waters to turbulent seas.
Acceptance, no judgment tender loving care.
The strongest of bonds softest warm breeze.
Loving arms reaching out cold night's despair.
Forever by your side trust never leaves.

☾ Loves Eternal Dance ☽

Thumps in my head such a terrible plight.
One dream upon another pray they come true.
Holding onto lamp posts frigid cold night.
Freedom is everything come make your debut.
A slice of heaven peaceful doves take flight.
I put on my wings forever renewed.

٭٭☾ Poetry From The Heart ☽٭٭

Let your intuition guide your way.
A beacon of wisdom wrapped in sweet grace.
Hissing static, a deafening maze.
Sift through the cloud's clear crystal vase.
Don't silence your ears will only dismay.
Trust your divinity soft silky embrace.

****☾ Loves Eternal Dance ☽****

Be my lover, be my friend.
I will give you the same love echoes return.
Two hearts once broken beautifully mend.
My hand in yours two sacred red ferns.
Souls of sweet purity lotus blossoms ascend.
Waited so long for you I do yearn.

☾ Poetry From The Heart ☽

Do you look at yourself in the darkest of nights?
Do you dig deep within without feeling singed?
Do you confront the darkness beholding the light?
Do you embrace the contrasts grays into white?
Do you love yourself soft woven fringe?

****☾ Loves Eternal Dance ☽****

Do you sometimes feel life is unfair?
Sunshine melts into fog when will it lift?
Mirrors reflecting such a harsh stare.
It's all an appearance dig deep for the gifts.
Your soul chooses things you never would dare.
Trust your divinity release the despair.

****☾ Poetry From The Heart ☽****

Look into my eyes what do you see?
I am an old soul my heart just knows.
Fighting in battles many deaths tragedies.
Pushed off a cliff became one with the sea.
Fizzing champagne ancient bubbles in snow.
Rebirthed once again I vow to be me.

☽ Loves Eternal Dance ☾

Healing takes time let yourself be.
Accept the setbacks, two steps back forward three.
Believe in yourself a miraculous gift.
Unique as a snowflake sweet baobab tree.
Celebrate small victories wrapped in a kiss.
Tick-tocking watch clocks just sail off adrift.

Poetry From The Heart

My toes in the water so soothing and calm.
Future horizons cast beautiful hues.
Believe in miracles soft soothing balm.
The impossible blossoms sweet shades of blue.
Do you know you hold heaven right in your palm?

☾ Loves Eternal Dance ☽

I hear your words whispering in my ear.
Soft white petals slowly open with grace.
So fragrant, so sweet blossoms so sheer.
I sail with my beloved dressed in fine lace.
Silky waters so still your love so sincere.
I close my eyes feel your tender embrace.

✶✶☾ Poetry From The Heart ☽✶✶

I see you I love you your soul filled with grace.
Be kind to your yourself give yourself an embrace.
Self-love the foundation for all that is great.
May it flow from your heart to the whole human race.
It's energy so strong will stomp out all hate.
Loving hands intertwined what a beautiful fate.

☾ Loves Eternal Dance ☽

The Universe impersonal it takes what you give.
Lyrics of beauty morph into sad songs.
Words of such power echoes definitive.
Change the trajectory no right or wrong.
Empowering choices no need to relive.
Feed it sweet music no need to forgive.

☾ Poetry From The Heart ☽

Believe you can heal even if you do not.
Your words have power tiny tugboats.
Your brain listens carefully but tied up in knots.
A primitive shadow cast doubt just devote.
Self-love is like magic not just a plot.
Whispers of hope words that just float.

☾ Loves Eternal Dance ☽

Love can move mountains so powerful so strong.
Love can breathe fire into the coldest of storms.
Love can heal so comforting and warm.
Love can erase hurts so tattered and torn.
Love can change humanity no need to mourn.

Poetry From The Heart

My quill and ink all dried up.
My head is hurting empty spaces of dust.
I grope for some meaning just a hiccup.
Most barren of deserts I need to adjust.
Float back in time Victorian teacup.
Let yourself be bathe in God's trust.

****☾ Loves Eternal Dance ☽****

It took me sometime to trust again.
Past words of love full of deception.
Then you came along so sweet and divine.
My heart feels your heart no more chagrin.
You melt me, excite me feels so sublime.
Warm fingers I tingle come be my Zen.

☾ Poetry From The Heart ☽

Your love penetrates down to my core.
Though distance between us never apart.
Our souls found one another it's you I adore.
I waited a lifetime to feel you, cherished heart.
Gentle waves in my ears I dream by the shore.
You wipe away my tears priceless French art.

☾ Loves Eternal Dance ☽

I hold my new mantra close to my heart.
A mind full of doubt wisp away all the fears.
A new dawn begins a time to restart.
My pain is not me, worn clothing in tears.
The softest of whispers rings in my ears.
"I will heal," she echoes, "I will never depart."

✶✶☾ Poetry From The Heart ☽✶✶

We live in a world upside down on its head.
Sometimes full of joy other times so much dread.
May more love blossom as wide as the sea.
Go deep within let the bigotry shed.
Cast away all the hate lets end misery.
Rivers of kindness sweet water's edge.

❨ Loves Eternal Dance ❩

Emotions a symphony of joy and despair.
Violins, cellos lightness morphs into gray.
A landscape of contrasts wet oceans desert air.
Currents wash over feeling swept away.
Let them flow through you lay your soul bare.
Feel the soft cleansing shimmering light rays.

☾ Poetry From The Heart ☽

Life is more than enduring and strife.
Bands so tight shattered moonlight.
Sometimes it feels like the sharpest of knives.
Please come tomorrow crystal daylight.
Faith whispers to me, "You'll have a new life."
On top of a mountain candlelit night.

☾ Loves Eternal Dance ☽

I know it's not easy to sit with the pain.
I know it's not easy to feel at unease.
I know it's not easy to bear all the strain.
I know it's not easy echoing pleas.
I know it's not easy harsh pelting rain.
I know it's not easy hope's not in vain.

☾ Poetry From The Heart ☽

I need you to hold me never let go.
I need your sweet arms embrace me so tight.
Let the tears come softly pristine white snow.
A kiss so tender I float to new heights.
I tingle, I quiver right down to my toes.
You whisper, "I love you; it will be alright."

****☾ Loves Eternal Dance ☽****

You think you can say whatever you please?
Quill and ink to paper words of love I do write.
So dark and vulgar falling poisonous trees.
You cannot take my power nor banish my light.
My voice you will hear bounce off the trapeze.
I am a Goddess, a warrior I float on calm seas.

✳☽ Poetry From The Heart ☾✳

Sometimes people are not who they seem.
You may think you know them crushed velvety dreams.
Your eyes look through lenses all blurry to me.
You do what you may just go to extremes.
I stand by your side my heart will not flee.
Masks made of rocks I set myself free.

☾ Loves Eternal Dance ☽

The bluest of eyes sunlight kisses your face.
Tranquil waves rolling gentle sea mist.
Your love hypnotizes blue aster lace.
I lay down beside you I cannot resist.
Touch me in ways sweet heavenly grace.
My soul touches yours a rapturous gift.

☾ Poetry From The Heart ☽

Sometimes things just don't feel right.
Trust your intuition step into the light.

☾ Loves Eternal Dance ☽

Wolves in sheep's clothing deceptive not rare.
Your friendship unwavering only a tale.
Betrayal cuts deep such a stark stare.
Thoughts not your own you didn't exhale.
Your voice silenced crushed stifling air.
I released you, I had to my soul is not frail.

☽ Poetry From The Heart ☾

Kindred souls reunited wrapped in twilight.
Reawakened by words poetically shared.
Two quills dipped in ink soft candlelight.
Mosaics softly woven crafted with care.
Light morphs into dark imaginations take flight.

☾ Loves Eternal Dance ☽

A strong loving woman holds magical keys.
A warrior, a goddess pure divinity.
Mystical, enchanting she rolls with the sea.
Frigid winters, scathing deserts unsung victories.
Walking in shoes ancient and worn.
Her sisterhood, her lineage black locust thorns

⟪ Poetry From The Heart ⟫

My words are just empty, unexpected surprise.
I go into that space so open so wide.
Vast vacant hollows dark symphonies rise.
My life is on hold I sit, and I hide.
Such an injustice my heart wants to cry.
I pray in my sorrow let faith be my guide.

****☾ Loves Eternal Dance ☽****

Let your voice be heard worth a thousand words.
Stand on a mountain top sweet Mother earth.
Do not be afraid boundaries unblurred.
Fearlessness floats know your own worth.
No trepidation beautiful songbirds

⁎⁎☾ Poetry From The Heart ☽⁎⁎

Sometimes love is very tough.
Life's twists and tangles doors closing shut.
Frustration as deep as a tearful sea.
Obstacles, limitations soaking wet bluffs.
My heart is sad weeping willow trees.
I give you my hand, it may not be enough.

☾ Loves Eternal Dance ☾

True friendship isn't a sport.
Not just a pastime a game of lacrosse.
Feelings are real, hurts cut like a knife.
Turning and twisting words that distort.
Your mask cast aside dizzying heights.
I now see you clearly, rock crystal quart

☾ Poetry From The Heart ☽

Let go of things you can't control.
Things start to change, people grow old.
Embrace all that is your wise and so bold.
The years are like gifts wrapped in fine gold.
Wisdom and courage blessings unfold.
Discover yourself not made from a mold.

☾ Loves Eternal Dance ☽

Sounds of anxiety ring in my ears.
Not always mine but another I deal.
Feels so contagious dark and severe.
Nervous system rattled will I still heal?
I fight for my sanity in a wisp disappear.
I pray to the Universe blessings revealed.

****☾ Poetry From The Heart ☽****

Buckets and buckets and buckets of tears.
No drops on my face in my heart sixteen years.
Choices we make not crystalline clear.
Some the wrong reasons borne out of fear.
I climb the staircase but isn't one here.
May I find my savior, my freedom is near.

⟪ Loves Eternal Dance ⟫

Trudging through sandstorms dust in my eyes.
My feet so heavy can't bear one more step.
I push through the aching azure blue skies.
Invisible spirits I feel with each breath.
They lift me, console me ever so wise.
Life's what you make it, not Russian Roulette.

☾ Poetry From The Heart ☽

My words tumble out sometimes with ease.
Other times searching stained visceral art.
They must be written strong winter breeze.
Pieces free falling all torn apart.
My essence, my being holds ancient keys.
I am who I am, a new dawn a new start.

☾ Loves Eternal Dance ☽

"A work in progress," yes, that is you!
The strong ones, the brave ones creating self-love.
Look deep within no fear of the views.
Symphonies of grace sacred grey doves.
Keep moving mountains reveal what is true.
Embrace your humanity sweet heaven above.

☾ Poetry From The Heart ☽

Believe in miracles they often appear.
Believe in hope broken hearts do repair.
Believe in magic a gift to be shared.
Believe beyond gazes rarefied air.
Believe all is possible tender loving care.

☾ Loves Eternal Dance ☽

Your love for me so passionate so rare.
Your kindness, you're caring a breath of fresh air.
My trust was in tatters you wrapped in such care.
My head in your lap sweet poetry in my ears.
You ignite my fire thoughts I never have dared.
Come take me, engulf me forever we share.

☾ Poetry From The Heart ☽

You flow like a river soft streams velvet air.
So easy, so tender is this magic or real?
You wake me from dreams tinged with despair.
Desires locked down deep canyons you've peeled.
Flames that ignite love naked and bare.
Gaze into my eye's vulnerabilities revealed.

✸✸☾ Loves Eternal Dance ☽✸✸

I fight my demons their unkindness their glare.
Put on my wings fly to sweet foreign lands.
I battle, I crawl, cold naked and bare.
Ancient brain lost buried hollows of sand.
Stubborn and frightened irrational demands.
Tell her she's safe, come take my hand.

☾ Poetry From The Heart ☽

Unconditional love, blue diamonds so rare.
Naked and raw I give you, my heart.
You embrace my suffering, my pain, my despair.
I let it sink in, baby blues don't depart.
You wrap me in arms full of such care.
I want you, please take me, never apart.

****☾ Loves Eternal Dance ☾****

When someone you love gets hit with despair,
Feeling so helpless my shoulders are strong.
You feel their pain tidal waves hard to bear.
I stand by your side just know you belong.
Don't listen to voices that quake without care.
Just know you are wrapped in heavenly songs.

Poetry From The Heart

Only one magic potion can set you free.
Dive into love true Divinity.

☾ Loves Eternal Dance ☽

Bathe yourself in love every day.
Divine soothing waters never leave you astray.
Embrace your Divinity, it will show you the way.

****☾ Poetry From The Heart ☽****

You come into my dreams then dash out of sight.
Was I really dreaming or awake at twilight?
I long for the day I feel your embrace.
A rebirth of love Monarch butterflies take flight.
Ascend murky waters lotus flowers sweet grace.
My quill dipped in ink I dream as I write.

٭٭☾ Loves Eternal Dance ☽٭٭

My words aren't magic they speak from my soul.
Sometimes so airy other times dark and bold.
Sometimes they tumble rolling weeds drift astray.
A mosaic of feelings splattered on a page.
Voices of contrast some hearts they take hold.
Some echoes are silent untouched on this day.

☽ Poetry From The Heart ☾

What do you do when the pain gets intense?
No magic tricks cast their spell won't pretend.
Try to distract crumbled leaves broken fence.
Float above clouds dare I levitate to mend?
Disappear into stardust may it relent.
My poetic words my savior, my friend.

☾ Loves Eternal Dance ☽

Love and grace such beautiful words.
An exquisite perfume lingering that stirs.
Scented from Godliness let their magic be heard.

☾ Poetry From The Heart ☽

Trembling words reflect inner tears.
Some things worth fighting for others not.
Pits in my stomach, splintered old stairs.
Sinking lifeboats torn off a yacht.
Dreaming of freedom do I even dare?
Hold tight sweet darling let go of the fears.

☾ Loves Eternal Dance ☽

Feeling lonely lost as blown winds.
Words of love just roll off my skin.
Hands to my ears stop the words feeling pinned.
A house with strangers a tormenting sin.
Sadness deep wells let it flow not rescind.
A new dawn upon us let it begin.

May I be blessed with grace to hold you.
May I look into your eye's calm sea of blue.
May I be reawakened soft murmuring coos.

****☽ Loves Eternal Dance ☾****

If my words were only sweetness and light,
Would you like them better a confection's delight?
All soft and bouncy trampolines satin skies.
Deeply exhale poetic droplets dark night.
A creature of contrasts will never disguise.
My joy is my sorrow upside down as I write.

☾ Poetry From The Heart ☽

Only love will set your soul free.
Let it flow from your heart ethereal light.
Kindness and compassion pure golden keys.
Angelic whispers inner angels take flight.

****☾ Loves Eternal Dance ☽****

Can you hold and kiss me all night long?
Come awaken my fire wipe away all the tears.
Fill me with rapture sultry love songs.
Read me some poetry sweetly tug at my hair.
Blossoming lotuses purr gently till dawn.

☾ Poetry From The Heart ☽

I put down my quill swan feathers so still.
Sad words escape me only feel it within.
No compromise just a bitter dark pill.
I seek only comfort soothing Mozart violins.
Life unexpected cold barren chills.
I do not seek empathy is that such a sin?

⚣ Loves Eternal Dance ⚣

Do you feel as if the next step is bare?
A staircase collapsing cold frozen tears.
Do you know where to go or just sit and stare?
Motionless in limbo deep breaths azure tears.
Your strength is boundless soft linen air.
Divinity always with you, have faith do you dare?

☾ Poetry From The Heart ☽

Laughter is heaven a gift from above.
Live in the moment sweet sacred doves.
Laugh till you cry surrender to love.

☾ Loves Eternal Dance ☽

To love you with every breath of my soul,
Would it penetrate deeply pure liquid gold?
Your heart I hold in the palm of my hand.
Mine nestled in yours the softest white sand.
Trust so sacred water lilies so grand.

✴✴☾ Poetry From The Heart ☽✴✴

Happiness can be fleeting cold winds autumn air.
Find joy deep within make friends with you soul.
Underneath all the rubble, anxiety, and tears,
Lives a house of Divinity to lift and uphold.
Speak to this wonder it is you not a care.
Eternally loved fulfilled everywhere.

☾ Loves Eternal Dance ☽

Your subconscious not all darkness and fear.
Your hidden angels also live there.
Contrasts of light and dark fill the air.
Your creativity whispers, "My love I am here."

☾ Poetry From The Heart ☽

Beauty comes in a myriad of forms.
Snowcapped mountains jewels in my eyes.
Natures sweet whispers God's miraculous songs.
Indigo oceans, baby blue skies.
In the eye of the beholder lenses not wrong.
Surrounded by treasures breathe in feel alive.

✶✶☾ Poetry From The Heart ☽✶✶

I can't wait to hold you to feel your touch.
Longings engulf me gazelles bathed in heat.
You make my heart sing I tingle and gush.
Your love an aphrodisiac my words barely speak.
Fires inside so warm but so plush.
Soul bared naked dripping chocolates so sweet.

☾ Loves Eternal Dance ☽

Why do so many have to live on the edge?
Scarcity of money, will there be food or a bed?
Is this a soul's choosing no way to discern?
So many people just need to be fed.
Loving hearts simple basics, they yearn.
Come let's join hands so much to learn.

Karma's not evil simply a law.
The Universe sends back what you give without flaw.
Be kind to others live in Gods' awe.

****☾ Loves Eternal Dance ☽****

Count your blessings every day.
Even if lack should come your way.
Look into small crannies see the light rays.
A smile from a stranger a deep loving heart.
Every dawn a God send, a brand-new start.

✴☾ Poetry From The Heart ☽✴

Try to be kind, not hard to do.
Make someone's day chase away all the blues.
Self-love the catalyst beautiful hearts open wide.
Spread love melted chocolate heavenly views.
Lift a spirit bestow them with pride.
Compassion and grace step into their shoes.

****☾ Loves Eternal Dance ☽****

I hold out my hand, take it it's yours.
We walk together rugged journeys harsh wars.
Hearts that sink deep ocean floors.
You're never alone, we'll transform shattered doors.

****☾ Poetry From The Heart ☽****

Do you trust or is it tattered and torn?
So many hurts, bleeding hearts no remorse.
Friends, lovers some leave you worn.
Healing sorrows untamed dark horse.
Rollercoasters dip alone and forlorn.
Turn away from the mirror look at the source.

☾ Loves Eternal Dance ☽

A new day begins, darkness morphs into light.
I open my eyes dripping cold frozen tears.
A child bewildered cannot grasp the fight.
Such discord alarming stained 17 years.
You change in a second, soft sun into night.
My faith must strengthen ascend golden stairs.

****☾ Poetry From The Heart ☽****

Faded images throughout the years.
Memories of wholeness just disappeared.
I will get back my life shackles worn out.
I will find peace again; I must have no doubt.

☽ Loves Eternal Dance ☾

Acceptance of others comes from your heart.
Open it like blossoms that beautifully part.

☾ Poetry From The Heart ☽

The sky is cloudy time ticks away.
Just give of your heart on this blessed day.
A smile so precious harsh winter storms.
The ice is melting your love gifted warmth.

☾ Loves Eternal Dance ☽

I think of my youth trips far away.
From the Far East to Europe,
Such glorious days.
I sit on my perch little bird lost in trance.
Float on a dream one day I will stray.
Trust in the future, "My love shall we dance?"

☾ **Poetry From The Heart ☽**

Can you look way deep into my eyes?
Are they full of sorrow or human flaws?
My heart wide open, cannot tell a lie.
Emotions splattered vulnerable and raw.
I like this place naked I fly.
Be at peace little darling find your "awe."

☾ Loves Eternal Dance ☽

May tender words flow from your lips.
May they heal a heart such a sacred gift.

☽ Poetry From The Heart ☾

I want to touch you.
Your lips close to mine.
Trusting hands holding hearts forever divine.

☾ Loves Eternal Dance ☽

Melting into your soul, it's you I adore.
Trust torn and shattered tenderly erased.
Shattered porcelain heart you picked off the floor.
Cradled in kindness soft silky embrace.
Your whispers of love I quake star lit shores.
Penetrate my longings lost in your grace.

☽ Poetry From The Heart ☾

Roaming across time and space.
Be kind to all beings God's divine grace.
Can we make this Universe a heavenly place?
Steeped in care, love the whole human race.

****☾ Loves Eternal Dance ☽****

May the heavens burst with love so divine.
Let your heart blossom, sweet buds on a vine.
We are all connected, our hearts bleed the same.
Can we all join hands, breaking bread as we dine?
We are not in this life for glory or fame.
Just live authentically humanity not a game.

☾ Poetry From The Heart ☽

You spew out your temper,
Volcanos bubbling, hot lava stings.
Tried so hard, trails burning embers.
Sadness on me, I will never cling.
A diamond so pretty, yellow like spring.
I cast it aside, imagination of splendor.

☾ Loves Eternal Dance ☾

Friendship a love so precious and dear.
Never take it for granted, it will just disappear.
Honor it, savior it, it must be revered.

⁂ ☾ Poetry From The Heart ☽ ⁂

Let me kiss away your sorrows.
Wipe away all your tears...
Your scars are my scars.
Throughout all the years.

⁕⁕☾ Loves Eternal Dance ☽⁕⁕

If my words could erase all your fears.
I would blow them to you, kisses so dear.
Climb on my shoulders, shed your sweet tears.

✷✷☾ Poetry From The Heart ☽✷✷

Look in the mirror, what do you see?
Can you see your beauty, or does it slip away?
Trauma, abuse, falling lost trees.
Reflections that lie, deceive, and betray.
Fun house mirrors lost stolen keys.
Self-love is your savior, set yourself free.

Loves Eternal Dance

Sitting alone in solitude.
What a divine feeling, a heavenly respite.
Surrounded by conflict of such magnitude.
A symphony of silence, a musical delight.
I gnaw my teeth, trenches of fortitude.
Soft whispers, I exhale, "It will be all right."

☽ Poetry From The Heart ☾

We go through heartaches, twists, and turns.
They are our mentors, please let us discern.
Your divinity is with you, so much to learn.

❨☽ Loves Eternal Dance ☾❩

Love is divinity kisses straight to the heart.
Open your gateways, let it flow right within.
Your light is eternal, just make a new start.
God breathes inside you, will never rescind.
Believe in pure magic, may your star never dim.

Don't miss out!

Visit the website below and you can sign up to receive emails whenever Teri Dourmashkin publishes a new book. There's no charge and no obligation.

https://books2read.com/r/B-A-QHNBB-RVCWC

BOOKS 2 READ

Connecting independent readers to independent writers.

Did you love *Love's Eternal Dance*? Then you should read *Elixir of Love*[1] by Teri Dourmashkin!

In "Elixir of Love: Versus To Mend the Soul," the poet invites readers to explore the depths of their hearts, to embrace their humanity with all its flaws and beauty, and to find solace and strength in love's transformative power. This collection is a tribute to the resilience of the human spirit, a celebration of the capacity to love and be loved, and an ode to the healing journey each of us undertakes in the quest for wholeness and fulfillment.

Read more at terilove.com.

---

1. https://books2read.com/u/mg5pkD

2. https://books2read.com/u/mg5pkD

About the Author

Dr. Teri Dourmashkin, Ed.D., is the founder of a minimalist skincare line, known for its natural ingredients and handcrafted batches. Alongside her skincare expertise, she is a passionate poet, blending beauty and wellness in both her professional and creative pursuits.terilove.com

Read more at terilove.com.